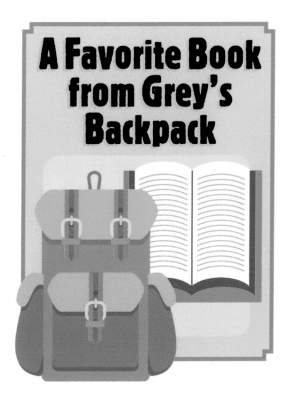

A Favorite Book from Grey's Backpack

Machines at Work

Police Cars

by Allan Morey

Bullfrog Books

Ideas for Parents and Teachers

Bullfrog Books let children practice nonfiction reading at the earliest reading levels. Repetition, familiar words, and photo labels support early readers.

Before Reading
- Discuss the cover photo. What does it tell them?
- Look at the picture glossary together. Read and discuss the words.

Read the Book
- "Walk" through the book and look at the photos. Let the child ask questions. Point out the photo labels.
- Read the book to the child, or have him or her read independently.

After Reading
- Prompt the child to think more. Ask: Where have you seen a police car? Where do you think it was going? What do you think happened?

Bullfrog Books are published by Jump!
5357 Penn Avenue South
Minneapolis, MN 55419
www.jumplibrary.com

Library of Congress Cataloging-in-Publication Data

Morey, Allan.
  Police cars / by Allan Morey.
    pages cm. — (Machines at work)
  Includes bibliographical references and index.
  Audience: K to Grade 3
  ISBN 978-1-62031-104-2 (hardcover) —
  ISBN 978-1-62496-172-4 (ebook)
Summary: "This photo-illustrated book for early readers explains the parts of police cars and how they help police officers do their jobs" — Provided by publisher.
  1. Police vehicles — Juvenile literature. I. Title.
  HV7936.V4M67 2014
  363.2'32—dc23
                                    2013039884

Series Editor: Wendy Dieker
Series Designer: Ellen Huber
Book Designer: Anna Peterson
Photo Researcher: Kurtis Kinneman

Photo Credits: All photos by Shutterstock except: Digitalstormcinema/Dreamstime, cover; Tom Robinson/Dreamstime, 2; Robert Harding Picture Library/SuperStock, 5; Roger Allyn Lee/SuperStock, 10; AKP Photos/Alamy, 10–11; Exactostock/SuperStock, 15; Michael Matthews-Police Images/Alamy, 16–17; Brett Critchley/Dreamstime.com, 16; Flickr, 18; Lostafichuk/Dreamstime.com, 20–21; i car/Alamy, 22; Gary Blakeley/Dreamstime.com, 24

Printed in the United States of America at Corporate Graphics, in North Mankato, Minnesota.
3-2014
10 9 8 7 6 5 4 3 2 1

Table of Contents

Police Cars at Work   4

Parts of a Police Car   22

Picture Glossary   23

Index   24

To Learn More   24

Police Cars at Work

Zoom!
A police car races by.

Officer Tim drives
the car.

Where is he going?

To stop a robber!

Warning lights flash.

They are red
and blue.

warning
lights

The siren is loud.

Wee-oo! Wee-oo!

Cars move.

They get out of the way.

The robber goes in the back seat.

The doors have no handles.

The robber can't get out.

Officer Bob works in his car.
It has a computer.

computer

He gets a report.

The car has a radio.

"A man needs help!"
Officer Bob hears.

"On my way!" he says.

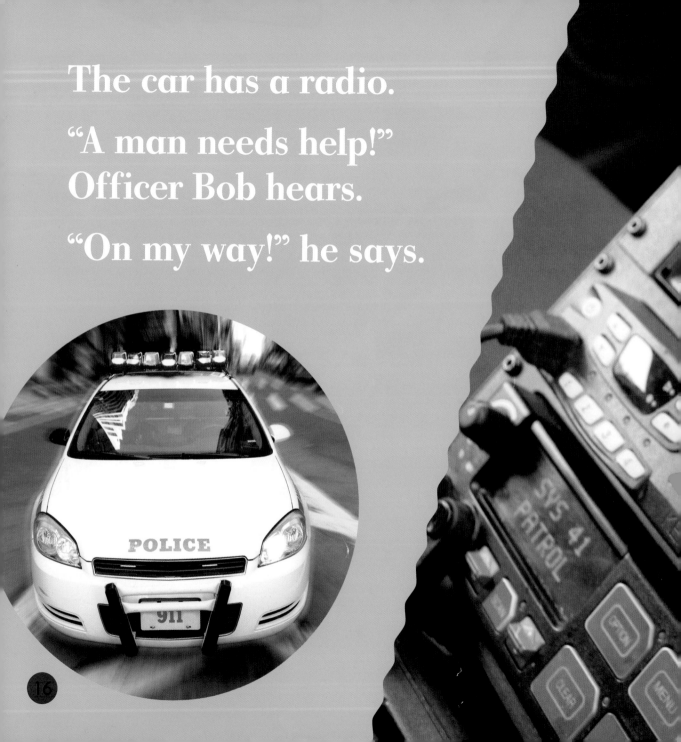

POLICE

911

SYS 41
PATROL

radio

The car has a trunk.

It is big.

first-aid kit

It holds safety gear.
There is a first-aid kit.

Police cars help officers do a good job.

Parts of a Police Car

camera
A device that records what happens while a police officer is on the job.

light bar
The bar that holds a police car's flashing lights.

spotlight
A light for shining into dark places.

push bumper
A strong bumper used to force other cars off the road.

Picture Glossary

computer
A machine that police officers use to look up information.

radio
A device used to tell police officers where they need to go.

first-aid kit
Bandages and medicines used to help people who have been hurt.

warning lights
Flashing lights that let people know a police car needs to get through.

Index

back seat 13

computer 14

first-aid kit 19

police officer
   7, 14, 16, 20

radio 16

report 15

robber 7, 13

siren 10

trunk 18

warning lights 8

To Learn More

Learning more is as easy as 1, 2, 3.

1) Go to www.factsurfer.com

2) Enter "police car" into the search box.

3) Click the "Surf" button to see a list of websites.

With factsurfer.com, finding more information is just a click away.